SPREA____ ____
WILD FLOWERS
Poems by Timothy Gager

Jess,

Live "24-7"

Tim

ISBN: 978-1-945917-58-5
Printed in the United States of America
Front Cover Photo: Timothy Gager

Also by Timothy Gager:

Chief Jay Strongbow is Real
The Shutting Door
Anti-Social Network
These Poems are not Pink Clouds
This is Where you go when you are Gone
We Needed A Night Out
The same corner of the Bar
Grand Slams: a coming of eggs story
The Thursday Appointments of Bill Sloan
Every Day There is Something About Elephants
Treating A Sick Animal: Flash and Micro Fictions
Short Street
Twenty-Six Pack
The Damned Middle: Life in a Drunken Slumber

BIG TABLE
Publishing

"Making other books jealous since 2004"

Big Table Publishing Company
Boston, MA & San Francisco, CA
www.bigtablepublishing.com

Reviews

ROBERT OLEN BUTLER "Timothy Gager is a genius of the quotidian, keenly observing the details of our lives and rendering them so that we can hear the deep pulse of our identities, of our pure being, within them."

AFAA M. WEAVER "Gager studies the crisp space between life's summation and the gathering of what harvest may wait for us as we work at a more genuine quality of being."

FRED MARCHANT "Worldly, witty, and often satirical, Gager's poems also have a tender side, a feeling of loss and longing, a sense of thwarted hopes and dreams."

JANUARY O'NEIL "Gager writes through the lens of a damaged angel, someone who has seen forgiveness from all sides. The result is wondrously eloquent, giving us these beautiful, dangerous, arresting poems about what it means to be human."

CHARLES COE "Timothy Gager mines gems of truth from the plain soil of ordinary life."

RUSTY BARNES "His eye for the telling detail remains, but his work has become more expansive, more timely, and less hard-bitten. This is a mature poet showing us exactly what he's got: and it's good."

Natural Creativity

SHAINDEL BEERS "Gager's poems that fight for truth and justice and love—whether we're ready for them yet, or not."

HARLYM 1TWO5 "Timothy's work is the cool that doesn't know it's fire. And his poetry, dry ice, cold to a flame. And all that cool, fire, ice, vocabulary and metaphor make volcanoes out of sandboxes of life and experience."

VI KHI NAO "The poems in this collection will drill quotidian sadness and nostalgia and hope into your left torso and make you dream of fabric softener and leggings and fertilizer."

For my mother

Introduction

Timothy Gager and I have seen a lot over the years in the local literary world. We started the The Somerville News Writers Festival (2003 to 2010), he ran the Dire Literary Series for almost two decades, and he published many works of short fiction and poetry. There is a consistent current flowing through this man's veins. That current keeps him writing, and expanding, both personally and professionally. No one can doubt his dedication to the craft; and what he has done for the literary community over the years.

I met Gager about twenty years ago. Back then he was a different man, a different poet, and a different writer. My small press, Ibbetson Street, published his first book of poetry, *The Same Corner of the Bar.* Now, twenty years later Gager is not in the same corner. On the front cover of his seminal book, one can see a hungover Gager—with a bottle of booze on his bed, and, beside him, a comely blonde in the midst of her drunken slumber. The older Gager I know now would be more likely looking through some nocturnal window—into the deep recesses of his own soul.

During those earlier years, Gager was a well-oiled alcoholic (which he makes no bones about revealing), was not in touch with himself, and was distracted from his surroundings. His poetry had a raw, Bukowski-style punch—with slivers of light around the edges. Gager, at that time was still fairly young—in his mid-30s—and was beginning his long road to recovery. The years have left an impact on his writing.

It occurred to me when I was reading his poem in *Ibbetson Street 45,* "In the Dark Corner of a Theatre" (which also appears in this collection), how nuanced and sensitive the piece is in which Gager uses intertwined hands as a balm and embeds them in the tangle of nature:

Our hands touched, craved
completeness of fingers
intertwined, growing

limb-like vines,
shielding old cracks
of a brick wall.

In April, the climbers
stay sparse—may we
forbid nature a minute longer?

May we be offered blooms of ivy?
so tender the cover,
so gentle it grows.

    In his new collection *Spreading Like Wild Flowers*, Gager strips down the poems to their essence. His ears attuned to nature—the way a bird chirps metaphors on a rainy day, or a feral cat screeches in the dead of night—Gager knows not to ignore it.

    In his poem "At a Cookout for Poets" he uses metaphor expertly with his contemplation of death—and his feelings about his mother's illness.

Inside, I imagine my mother's kidney,
is like the old clove of garlic
in the host's refrigerator—
The tumor growing like its root,

pretending, to play polite here,
not to be intrusive, I will ask
God to take care of all
that is rotten.

Gager is a poet engaged—with the world, and his interiority—and we're grateful he shares his insights with us.

~ Doug Holder/Ibbetson Street Press
Lecturer in Creative Writing/Endicott College

Table of Contents

CONCERTO

I became lost in the bell curve,
which a saxophone's note made

me contemplate: please stay present
because I found this watching out

for snakes is something celebrated.
Will you ponder a geometrical illusion?

Area and circumference?
The formulas? Always the formulas.

Lips which suck a reed are thrown down,
either worthy at music, worthy at math,

unlucky at cards; not timorously,
we spread out our old comforter.

THIS POEM IS LIKE A BRUISE

This poem is like a bruise.
A deep black Lake of Superior knocking over
the white caps rolling into their last breaths.

It's an angry purple from the rage of red,
until the flattening of color blends
into the subdued yellow of surrender.

If you're weak of mind
this poem is not a holiday;
it does not twinkle, nor

are its words lights from a city,
observed upon the descent—
each, a pushpin of hope.

If you wait, there is just a tiny ripple
when a coin is flipped into a well.
Hollow is the eye-socket, dark, and empty.

IN THE DARK CORNER OF A THEATER

Our hands touched, craved
completeness of fingers,
intertwined, growing

limb-like vines,
shielding old cracks
of a brick wall.

In April, the climbers
stay sparse—may we
forbid nature a minute longer?

May we be offered blooms of ivy?
So tender the cover,
so gentle it grows.

BROMLEY'S FUNERAL HOME

The old suit jacket's pocket,
housed a tatty funeral card
I pulled out some life
after death, shuddered,

seeing your face creased
on a piece of wrinkled cardstock—you were
so young, but the memory so ancient.
Bromley inserted a few lines

from an ancient Catholic Prayer
printed over a clichéd picture:
Heaven's light beaming down.
Or is it shining up? I can't question this,

or understand a damned thing
about the day of your funeral.
The picture now worth less than
a thousand words unsaid.

SHAME

As sunlight squawked once more,
a rooster conned the night

again, waking to repulsion
of head from pillow.

Your eyes open like linen curtains,
with 'how-long' dust on the ruffle.

This morning's hair
stands like a million

which-a-way blades of grass,
needing to be mowed today;

green, growing, enriched, withdrawal.
It is my lushness, of recollection.

THE LAST TIME I SAW YOU

I left at 6 A.M.
The loser birds sang out

my name—my name—my name.
Nothing personal, I said.

WORDS, you had said I said
out loud in my sleep.

You said, "I won't see you again,"
I a little slurry, earlier that night

after you rode me to sanity
in ten forlorn minutes,

you cried recalling,
a tree limb falling

into your childhood bedroom.
Then hours after, snorting and sniffing

cocaine, the darkness dripped in.
Your house smelled of a hundred dead mice

decomposing, or an acrid gas leak stench
I identified with—sitting on a keg, that blows.

Six months later, I heard you lived in N'Orleans,
married an unveiled version of me, with all my "yets"

still to come, worse than all those
wretched "nows." I feel I can't stop

from mourning you, or the sidewalks
from cracking, my stumble toes catching

that uneven place where elm roots
raise the concrete higher.

THE HEART IS A BROKEN LITTLE THING

After you bounced it off a wall
you noticed, it didn't have feathers,
it didn't fly, it didn't soar.

It only thudded, leapt a bit,
rolled, and zig zagged,
then stopped beating—
died on the ground.

Removed from the host,
the heart is un-lasting.
Now, it is free.

FINDING THE BEAUTY

In a bar
two seats

are taken out of
every three, coats
in-between, each

one open stool
for only silence

between the couple
next to me tonight
she turned

saw her lips
soft, and filled

like the old pillow
I sunk my head into
fifteen years ago

I would have
written a poem

in my head- while
I drove home

tonight, it got up and left.

IMPAIRMENT AND LOSS

(*You cannot*)
Cannot see
Cannot see straight
Cannot see at all
Cannot see a difference

between miss you
or miss your face.
There's the difference

between two perfect squares;
expanding parenthetic
(brackets)
Today there are boundaries.

COLLEGE DINING HALL

Like Jesus, the school produced every Friday
        Fish, bread and macaroni and cheesy spinach squares

to feed the multitudes, but we had to
        add five shakes of salt for flavor,

force it down till the sun didn't shine.
        But, the next time it did I held up the shaker,

forming a prism decorating a girl beautifully like
        David Bowie's album cover, the gal insane,

the bread just a loaf of Wonder that,
        I planned to steal and she followed me—

 A temporary pillar
        of impermanent salt,
                home.

THE MIRACLES OF RECOVERY

The body experiences
the mind bending, I was lost

in a body

my mind bent

in such new shapes,
such tension before it snaps.

Who would have thought salvation is no longer
found in the piss jars in old isolated bedroom?

the mind snaps

the body

quakes its resistance.
I am one step away from

being pushed
in a wheelchair

when my body fails

the mind

perhaps just wilts
as a petal, the rose might—

we are all the stem, we salvage
ourselves from this withering.

A CERTAIN WARRIOR

I knew you when you were a broken
twig snapped under the feet of a boy

you knew; when it was time to leave
it was not too soon, not soon enough

every time, scars continued to grow, build
like tar in the lungs of a chain smoker

eventually, you were frozen
descending, sunk like a heavy iron

lung, filled by a diaphragm
and muscles never forget

to force air out of you
your head outside

your body on a bed
inside the steel tank

When you found strength
to go, or stay, to disentangle

the psychological knots
you climbed out of the known

straightened the alcoves and clefts
of your psyche, when you left

yet, you stayed, you are
able to do both, or either,

or anything-
            Sugar
                        Baby
                                    God.

NEARSIGHTEDNESS

as strong winds lift
the unfastened

off the ground,
you barely notice

what races beneath me—
when we saw lust,

wept at completion again,
propelled yourself as an arrow

toward me, such force
I thought for the split

second you made a point
that impaled my cornea—

my vision weakened suddenly
as dust kicking up like thick smoke,

the gust which can't diffuse
only makes it denser.

WHEN I FIND YOU IN AN OLD DIARY

What do I say to
the rainfall today?

I told it to quiet down,
couldn't hear myself think,

and, I didn't like what I read,
my eyes burning from sentiment.

What do we write when
we don't like anything?

I said, I wanted change, but
couldn't argue with the weather,

or stick around for the storm, either,
choosing not to remain stationary,

nor run away like the cows choose to.
Today, I run straight into a hurricane,

effectively, like a buffalo.

I REMEMBER
Autumn 1967

I met my Aunt during a year I had redacted.
She planted kisses on me, many years after
the incident, I can smell her fragrant lipstick,
felt her waxy smudges on my cheeks.

She knew she had forced
her way into my suffocation,
while the rest of the family laughed at
the hugs and kisses for me, the vacant boy,

squirming and flailing like someone
coming out of anesthesia,
or licking an electrical cord
I swore would provide relief.

I don't want to re-experience
those flashes to darkness,
but back in that moment, I felt tiny
and useless as the dust in a corner,

while the big fat elephant in the room,
howled with the rest of them.
They had silenced my screams
years earlier, but no one knew,

why I grew up so visceral,
imagining bashing all those faces,
all those laughing lips bleeding,
1...2...3...4...5...99...100,000

times you can't edit, but,
I can live with myself, a dead boy,
      who's a man lucky to start breathing,
            lucky I don't ever need
                  to forget that.

TOSSING THE MURDER WEAPON

Once we had a life
we can't go back to.

We had a something until
we lost it. That's a privilege,

we didn't see: gratitude,
and truth. Now it's a secret

we threw away. It will be easy,
But we won't get any further,

disappointment in living
in this very Oldsmobile,

parked on top of the bridge,
two hundred feet above a river.

There's 2.5 seconds of doubt
whether it will hit the water,

less doubt on whether it would be found—
divers won't look for a single weapon,

used for $10,000, hardly worth
the look in the poor sucker's eye.

The cars passing think we're only broken
down, perhaps urinating over the side.

No time to think what we have going down
Happening quick, the 2.5 plus 10 extra tics

to toss a gun, walk, don't run back to the car.

PENGUINS

Often we cast-off
lovers, then we try

living in the Artic.
Just try that, try

staying indoors with only
keep-sake wind-up toys,

stuffed animals, plastic figures.
All of these penguins I love.

I'll wear the penguin necktie,
the many friends on my torso.

Yet, I wind up alone
eating calamari and krill

so many times. Each
year, the female leaves.

I have no eggs to sit on.
The penguins know this.

FEAR. GOD BLESS MY SOUL

Your world flooded
disrupted, Dear God,
are we having a relapse now?
Remember, no resentments
toward mental states.

Just sit at home
as the tornado roars.
Just a vessel which love
throws against our homes.
Meditate on the crystals,

feel the windows
implode, just wait
to lick the glass off
the ground, Dear God, I am afraid,
like the gray cat, the stray, I've saved.

I am afraid.

The water will rise up
to a lightbulb. Your idea
I'm reaching for, like a bottle
of water I never used to want
to die, I only thought I did.

DAY ONE: THE DAY AFTER

One eye closed, in dysfunctional
disfigurement, and hardly staring,
"please don't look," willing to

accept—we sailed in open
seas, invited trouble, waved
on in whomever it was

when you felt lonely, but you bled,
screamed, *"What did I take?"* until
it ended in the demolition.

Your mother came over
for a search mission,
picking up the pieces,

the compounds of powders off the rug,
and kitchen floor, each one was a broken day.
"Were they drugs?" mother asked.

You answer with a self-righteous,
"Yes, dammit," with a fist, on the table.
Potentially, all hands will become disfigured.

What's the answer
when the question disappeared?
When it appears in rehab,

it is answered in the shame of 24 hours or 29 day.
The shame, not the no shame.
The shame, not the no shame.

BRINGING A MONKEY TO WORK

Procrastination was his name
He arrived on your back.

"We've reigned cats and dogs
here: never a monkey."

.

"Careful, you tell the boss, he
might rip off your hypocrisy."

Now you're facing the music.
Human Resources said,

"No one is allowed to throw feces
around this office. It's unfit for human

employment." You should leave.
The monkey will always be with you.

STILL THERE ARE BOXES

If only we let go, still
 images remain.
Pictures, photos fell
off the wall. The boxes?

Leave them there,
the many only enjoy being
trapped in a room full of people.
It's the way a cage works.

What provides the shade?
There's still a single hair standing
between my eyebrows like
a tree parching in the desert.

THE TRUTH ABOUT PASTELS

Fearless souls live deep
but wish for pastels, really,

soft in comparison, pigment
to soothe the seriously intolerant,

seeking to spring out of skin
as oily as Craypas. How difficult

to understand that sakura
are cherry blossoms, the name

outside the box. Inside is the task.
Feel free not to shun any of them.

HISTORIC NIGHT OF JULY 4, 2019

The bills piled up on my basket,
a feral cat yells in the night.

What have we have paid for today?
The tanks behind the fences?

The new Hitler wants
to be marbleized—already he is

who we thought he was!
If you want to crown him, crown him:

King Richard II, not Shakespeare,
authored his own downfall.

Veracity is a disparaging
catcall which chivvies

without brevet; the King
fancied himself Odysseus,

a cunning hero, sans the bootstrap
as the rain fell down on the cat's meow.

JURISPRUDENCE
After Las Vegas

Thoughts and prayers
are not enough
to solve this.

and having the same dialogue for
this assassin—what if he had
a sword, a car, a bomb?

See it's the same? To defend one-self,
to *carry* or just to carry on.
Money first, Amendment second,

our victim's right
to ask *not to be killed*,
then can we move forward?

Like in the children's game, Mother, *May I?*
It is mandatory to plead as
we are forced to move backward.

DEBATE ABOUT GUNS, TRUCKS AND TIMOTHY MCVEIGH
After Parkland, after Vegas, after Newtown, Sandy Hook, El Paso, Dayton, after...

When guns are outlawed, I will become an outlaw.
A fugitive-bandit-desperado-crook.
The over-under, it's a semi-automatic
conclusion: 604 to 17.

Fugitive, bandits, desperados, crooks.
Compare and carry fatal apples to lethal oranges
conclusion: 604 to 17.
We all gotta eat, right?

Comparing and carry fatal apples to lethal oranges.
Ammonium nitrate, switchblades, scalpels, blades.
We all gotta die, right?
Impulse to understand triggers,

ammonium nitrate, switchblades, scalpels, sharps.
The over-under, it's a semi-automatic
impulse to understand triggers.
When guns are outlawed, I will become an outlaw.

CENTRALIA. PENNSYLVANIA

It's smoldering
under the surface

unknown if this is
hell on earth

like Atlantis burning
all seeming so wrong.

People paint the highway
with penises and racism

slogans proclaiming the love of
swastikas or Joanie loves Chachi—

Herb loves Albert,
is not acceptable, but

a flaming cross might be?
Who knows these days

Orange man is blistering,
the people are moved,

the smoke seen when it's cold outside
the cracks obvious to the rest of the country.

Centralia might smolder for centuries.
The coal continues to ignite.

RED BARN

there is no reason
to go inside the Red Barn.
No need.
Suspicion.
Perception.

How we turn
will make America
want to call it as it is:
Blood on a meat hook
hanging from an adversary.

FAITH

I'm old enough to have dead friends,
And friends with dead friends,
And friends' dead Parents,
         dead Children, dead Spouses.

Month old Babies
die, I don't believe,
     we will ever see their ghosts.
And if we did, would they stop our hearts?

And would this heart still thrust blood
against opposite walls?

I wonder why
everything has to be.
And I'll never wonder,
if we will go on forever.

And I believe,
one day, I will close my eyes,
to pray—for nothing horrific to happen,
again and again until the very last breath.

A NIGHT BEFORE CHRISTMAS

When lips parted
We'll never have Paris,
We'll have trouble and love
sore muscles
tensed to spring
unhinged hinges, these knots
unlike the other nots-
the once upon a time
the happily ever after
the no, not never, not
ever to talk about.

AT A COOKOUT FOR POETS

Outside, I invent haikus,
fake free verses or laughter
about what's on the grill,
and significant other things.

Inside, I imagine my mother's kidney,
is like the old clove of garlic
in the host's refrigerator—
the tumor growing like its root,

pretending, to play polite here,
not to be intrusive, I will ask
God to take care of all
that is rotten.